712 MORE

THINGS TO WRITE ABOUT

BY THE SAN FRANCISCO WRITERS' GROTTO

INTRODUCTION BY PO BRONSON

CHRONICLE BOOKS

SAN FRANCISCO

CONTRIBUTORS

Seth Amos
Marie Baca
Tom Barbash
JD Beltran
Elizabeth Bernstein
Jenny Bitner
Liza Boyd
Po Bronson
Monica Campbell
Chris Colin
Molly Colin
Chris Cook
Michael Coren
Lindsey Crittenden
Mark Decena
David Duncan
Laura Fraser
Alastair Gee
Susie Gerhard

Melanie Gideon
Connie Hale
Rachel Howard
Vanessa Hua
Susan Ito
Zahir Janmohammed
Gerard Jones
Holly Jones
Yukari Kane
Diana Kapp
Lee Kravetz
Rachel Levin
Connie Loizos
Stephanie Losee
Kimberley Lovato
Kathryn Ma
Laura McClure
Kirsten Menger
Louise Nayer

Janis Newman
Zahra Noorbakhsh
Caroline Paul
Susanne Pari
Bridget Quinn
Cathryn Ramin
Jason Roberts
Ethel Rohan
Lorraine Sanders
Julia Scheeres
Lavinia Spalding
Bonnie Tsui
Fred Vogelstein
Meghan Ward
Ethan Watters
Maw Shein Win
Matthew Zapruder
Maury Zeff

ISBN: 978-1-4521-3263-1

Manufactured in China.

Designed by Tatiana Pavlova.

10 9 8 7 6 5 4 3 2 1

Chronicle Books LLC
680 Second Street
San Francisco, California 94107
www.chroniclebooks.com

Write an Introduction to this book.

Imagine you have enrolled in a creative writing class in the local college's adult extended-education program. You're not going to be graded; you're there just to learn. It's the first night of class. You took a seat in the second row. You don't know anyone.

The very first thing the teacher does is give the class a five-minute free-writing assignment, which you will read aloud to the class when you're done. Here's the prompt:

"Something you used to do that you no longer do."

Go.

An idea—of that thing you used to do—pops into your mind. But as you pick up your pen, you start to wonder if perhaps a better idea is just around the corner. A second idea is suddenly there. It's indeed a better idea . . . but, oh—you're not sure that's a subject you want to read aloud to strangers. Now your mind is warmed up, it's generating many ideas, and each of them you are simultaneously evaluating for whether it is better than the others. You keep returning to that second idea, the embarrassing and revealing one. Do you dare?

A minute has passed. Four minutes to get it on paper.

Creativity is defined as the production of something both novel and useful. So it requires uniqueness, yet also must be somehow appropriate to the given context. It can't just be a totally crazy idea—it has to be one of those crazy ideas that isn't so crazy after all. In the mind, this takes blender pulses of divergent thinking and convergent thinking, as you generate ideas and evaluate them.

And now, sitting there in class with pen to page, you repeat the blender pulses for every single sentence. You could start the sentence this way or that way—which is best? Faster, you think; just write. But no sentence escapes its cycle; even if you don't touch or edit the words hitting the page, the mind spins and sees other ways it could be composed. You toss these thoughts out just as fast as new ideas flow in. This is the state of writing.

Here are 712 more things to write about. We've realized, since our first book (*642 Things to Write About*), that we needed a higher concentration of prompts that you could actually complete in five to 10 minutes. In that sense, they needed to be more useful to this context. Yet they still needed the playful element that provokes the mind to dance and pulse. Not all are like this— just more of them, proportionately.

Enjoy,

PO BRONSON
San Francisco Writers' Grotto

Write yesterday's horoscope.

Your partner writes a Craigslist ad to get rid of an item of yours that they totally hate. What does it say?

A thank-you note for a weekend visit where everything went wrong

It's winter, and you have just moved to North Dakota. Write a postcard that makes Californians jealous.

Imagine you are on Yelp. Write a review of the restaurant everyone is talking about. In the fourth paragraph, admit you've never eaten at the restaurant, but argue why your misinformed opinion is still more important than the other reviews on the site.

A friend of yours at the NSA calls. She says that for just one hour, she will let you listen to the conversations of any two people in the world. You accept. Whose conversations do you listen to and what do they say? Transcribe them here.

You are a coach who has just cut an 11-year-old girl from the team.
Write an e-mail to her parents, explaining why.

Now you are the school principal. Write an e-mail to the coach who
cut the girl from the team, explaining why he is being fired.

Briefly but convincingly, explain why world peace is better
than indoor plumbing.

Just as briefly and convincingly, explain why indoor plumbing
is better than world peace.

Write a poem in the voice of Sylvia Plath on
antidepressants.

Write about something that is true at first light,
false by noon.

Write a ransom note.

Remarkably, a magazine all about you is launched. Write a letter to the editor.

The postcard's from a distant country.
The postmark on the stamp is local.

Let's say that Mel Brooks was right
and there were originally 15 Commandments. (Moses dropped five of them,
according to Brooks.) What are
Commandments 11 through 15?

What does the Magic 8 Ball say?

A fan note to a celebrity chef,
requesting a recipe for your parents'
50th wedding anniversary

You're playing truth or dare with yourself. What's the one truth you'd be afraid to tell, and the one dare you'd be afraid to act out?

"Lather. Rinse. Repeat." Adapt these famous how-to-use instructions for a new brand of shampoo for young males.

Write a list of your 10 favorite doors. Where do they lead?

Wonder Woman decides to get a haircut. Why?

A video posted of a singing child goes viral a year after it was posted. Talent agents begin calling her parents, but the child is now a runaway. What do the parents tell the callers?

Write a recipe for the world's most expensive cocktail, and give it a name.

What did the cat drag in?

You are a giant. What's on your to-do list today?

Write a list of the streets in your neighborhood. Use those to create five character names.

Describe a year from your life in a series of 52 tweets (140 characters each).

Write an e-mail from a 25-year-old man, asking his father
for money.

Write an e-mail from a 65-year-old man, asking his son for money.

Write an application letter to a new preschool for your son. Without being overt, you must somehow address why you have been asked by his old school to find a new school for him.

Write a recommendation letter for someone who is applying to graduate school—and who you don't actually think should be admitted.

Write about how shallow people try to create an aura of authenticity
by consuming books, films, and food, and befriending other, actually
authentic people.

List all the excuses you've heard people use this week.
Include ones from newspapers, radio, television, and
overheard conversations.

You've been afraid to tell your best friend
something for seven days. Write the scene in
which the truth comes out.

Observe the qualities of the air in three distinct locations—
at an open window, in a car, near a factory. Write a paragraph
about each, in the style of a wine critic.

One of your college buddies is a famous golfer. He violated the rules in a big tournament, but nobody spotted it. He calls you that night. Write the dialogue of the phone call.

You just realized you left something at home that you really need today. What is it?

This is the e-mail you accidentally sent to the wrong person.

You are a private investigator, hired by a mother to follow her daughter. What is the thing you decide not to report back to her?

Think of a food or cuisine you really dislike. Take a moment to
contemplate some aspects that turn you off. Now write about that
food from the point of view of someone who absolutely loves it.
Describe the dish in detail.

Write the names of five people you've been jealous of.

Over the course of the school year, a sixth-grade teacher intercepted
dozens of notes being passed between students. He keeps them in a drawer.
On the last day of school, he decides to read some of them. What do they say?

Imagine a packaged pastry product. Write a list of its ingredients, three quarters of which are synthetic chemicals like stiffeners and derivatives. Make up their names—the crazier, the better.

A woman rushes out of a house (not her house) to her car. On her car windshield, tucked under the wiper blade, is a handwritten note. What does it say?

Your job is to write catalogue copy for a company that sells home décor and bedding products. Write two descriptive entries, each 50 words or less, for two sets of bedsheets. One set sells for $59, the other for $129.

This text message pops up on your phone. It's from a friend telling you to meet her at the bar at 10:00 p.m. AutoCorrect has changed some words. How does the text read?

List the items in your college fridge.

Write a note to be posted in your office bathroom.

Your pet has one request of you.

You've called in to a customer service line, and you're getting
frustrated. Write one page of back-and-forth dialogue between yourself and the customer service representative. Push the boundaries.

A school principal's personal to-do list

A mortician's personal to-do list

A billionaire money manager's personal to-do list

This is the error message your laptop displays after you visited a
website about government secrets.

This is the bedside prayer your character whispers the night her
husband finally resurfaced.

Invent a band name.

Name a new children's toy.

Come up with the title of a new TV series.

What's in the table of contents of your breakfast cookbook?

Write about the three most important ingredients
in your cookbook.

What do you say to your cat or dog when you first encounter
the pet upon returning home?

....

....

....

....

....

....

....

....

....

....

The best meal I ever ate on a vacation

....

....

....

....

....

....

....

....

....

....

Write a text message to someone you
are about to meet for the first time,
describing what you look like so the
stranger will spot you in the crowd.

What does your tattoo message to your
older self say?

You've long suspected that your best
friend is a CIA operative. Now your child
is in danger overseas, and you need help.

Your cat (or dog) has a Twitter feed.
What are its first three tweets?

What were you thinking the first time you made out with someone?

List your favorite childhood games: hot lava monster, freeze tag,
hide-and-seek. Write a scene where adults play it.

Describe your home or apartment as though it were a potential
vacation destination.

Explain the derivation of one of the playing card suits:
Hearts, Spades, Clubs, or Diamonds. Make it up.

You're standing in your living room with a gun in your hand. A man
is lying dead on the floor. What happened?

It's the first time you've seen snow. Why does it make you cry?

Some people are embarrassed by _____ but I'm not because _____.

Write about a failed attempt to revive a family ritual.

If a toilet could pray, what would it pray for?

A paragraph about the imagined personal life of your first-grade teacher

How do you make Snoofaroo?

Write a story with this as the first line: *I sent another letter to Violet Finneran's son.*

When did you know that you'd fallen out of love?

Write the two lines you would send to a newly discovered
extraterrestrial population—the first ever communication
with them—to describe earth and the human population.

Recall one thing that your grandmother or grandfather taught you how to do, like brush your hair at night, make marinara sauce, cast for trout, sail a boat. Now write a letter to your grandchild, passing on that skill.

You have decided to fake your own death. How will you do it?

Now that you're falsely dead, write about how you will live your
new life and identity.

The three women who live next door to you remind you of the three witches in *Macbeth*. Why?

A moral dilemma in 100 words or less

Your sister has just told your parents she is gay, and she's upset by how they took the news. What do you say to comfort her?

Finish this telegram: "DEAR WIFE STOP ROUGH VOYAGE AT SEA STOP . . ."

It's your last day on Earth. You're in good health. How do you spend it?

Write the college application essay you wish you could have
written, being totally honest about the things you truly valued
at age 17 or 18.

Write about what it would feel like to get beaten up without
describing physical pain.

The Classics tell us of the nine Muses who inspire epic poetry, love poetry, music, oratory, dance, tragedy, comedy, history, and astronomy. Less well known are Muses 10 through 18. What do they inspire?

You're walking in a cemetery and discover a weathered tomb-
stone with your name on it. The person died a hundred years
ago. Who was the person?

Write a letter to someone you have haven't talked to in years about how your priorities have changed since you last met.

Consider a person you dislike and write a scene in which they lose their beloved dog.

Your boss and admired mentor tells you he needs your help covering up a scandal. What's the scandal, and how do you react?

A blind man who is obsessed with buttons

You are the inspiration behind a new cocktail. What is it called, and what's in it?

Ways that you and your father are alike

_____
_____
_____
_____
_____
_____
_____
_____
_____
_____

Write a scene that shows jealousy between you and one
of your siblings.

_____
_____
_____
_____
_____
_____
_____
_____
_____
_____

Who's the least funny person you know? Write out a joke as that person would tell it.

A woman walks into the ocean in a red ball gown

List your mother's favorite phone topics.

List your father's favorite phone topics.

You're on a flight from Dallas to Atlanta. You reach into the pocket attached to the seat in front of you, and you find a handwritten note. What does it say?

Write dialogue in which one person proposes marriage, and the other says no.

Write down all of the most disgusting words you've ever
heard and could never imagine using. Then write a diatribe
using all of them.

An argument via text message

I feel most alive when I'm . . .

Write about life in a hospital at two in
the morning.

The one thing you wouldn't want anyone to
know about you in this moment.

You have a chance to celebrate your 21st birthday again. What kind of party would you have and who is on your invitation list?

Rant for 10 minutes, starting with, "What sucks is . . ."

Describe your walk to school or
work from the point of view of
. . . a very drunk person.

. . . a very angry person.

. . . a very sleepy person.

. . . a very heartbroken person.

You are driving home in blinding rain from a hiking trip in a southern region of Texas. It's very late, and there is no one for miles on the dark country road. Suddenly your car dips into a very deep puddle, stalls, and then stops. You have no way of calling anyone. After a while, you see headlights approaching. An old pickup pulls up right behind you and stops. But no one gets out.

Tell the story of one of your scars.

Think about the word *vast*. What in your life is vast?

You are in a rickshaw in India. The driver asks if it's true that
there is a pill for everything in your country.

A man who disguises himself as an electrician

Write a proposal for why your favorite book should be made into a movie.

You have an opportunity to fly a blimp emblazoned with a message over a baseball field during a game. What will the message say?

Write five phrases that express regret.

Why is your 11-year-old son obsessed with lemurs?

Describe your favorite boss and what he or she taught you.

You're at the dog park and a very attractive fellow dog walker approaches you. By the end of your conversation, you have scheduled a beach date for the next day. You both arrive at the beach with your dogs—but they don't get along.

Complete this phrase six
times without mentioning
the sky or water:
"as blue as _____."

What does your character's
bumper sticker say?

You've awoken from a
nightmare in which the
person you love most did
horrific things.

You go to the store
hungry. You see apples and
peaches. Which one do you
choose and why?

Describe the oldest thing currently in your fridge.

You are a cowboy poet. Pen an ode to your hat.

Write a letter to your mother-in-law saying all the things you would never dare say to her face.

A woman has just chopped down a tree in front of her neighbor's house because the birds that live in it "are driving her mad." Her neighbor, who planted the tree 30 years ago in honor of his dead mother, arrives home just as the tree falls. Ten minutes later, he is seen with the woman's chain saw. What happened?

Write a brief obituary for an inanimate object near you.

In your yard is a sign that says "URGENT: Do not leave the house today." The handwriting is yours, but you have no recollection of writing it. What do you do?

You're a member of a casual carpool and it's your day to drive. A total
stranger gets into your car.

Shut your eyes. Make a mental note of the first five things you notice: sounds, sensations, smells, random thoughts. Write them down, then write for 10 minutes incorporating those five things.

Put a slave-owning
Mississippi plantation
farmer in a room with a Nazi
concentration camp guard.

Write a disassembly
manual for a relationship,
Ikea-style.

Your favorite beach

Read a long magazine article from a
good magazine. Then write one phrase
that summarizes each paragraph.
Arrange the phrases in a list to
see, at a glance, how the article
is structured.

A man walks out into a day with the intention of saying yes to every social
offer that he receives.

A UPS driver drops off a package at the home of a 36-year-old woman. Thirty minutes later, she is leaving her home, never to return. What's in the one duffle she takes with her?

Your outlook on life, written as an advertising slogan

What does a grandmother smell like?

List things that make you sweat.

She wanted it nice and tidy.

They slept on the kitchen floor.

He stayed at the Rowen Clinic.

She read the note, folded it, and nudged it with her foot into the gutter.

A man is furious with himself for leaving home without his cell phone,
but profound adventures unfold throughout the day because of it.

You've just received a lengthy e-mail from your college sweetheart whom you haven't seen in 20 years. He tells you about his life and wants to know about yours. Back when you were together, he moved to your college town to be with you—then left two weeks later after you dumped him for someone else (who later dumped you). It's clear he wants to meet and reconnect with you. Write about your subsequent correspondence and meeting.

The best shower you ever took

He didn't realize _____
until it was too late.

You spend a week on a train that
travels at the speed of light.
When you disembark, it is one
hundred years into the future.
Describe what you see.

What's one question you'd like
to ask your great-grandfather?

Your parents are celebrating their 50th wedding anniversary, and you found out
last night that your dad's been cheating. Write your toast.

Record a few minutes of dialogue between two characters from a
television sitcom, then transcribe it. Notice the texture—the
rhythm, cadence, choppiness of the exchange. Then create your
own scene, mimicking the texture of the recorded dialogue.

Think of three cities you have visited. Imagine three things
that are happening in each of those cities right now, and
write them down.

A death at a birthday party

If Abraham Lincoln time-traveled to present-day America, what would he think?
Describe his first few days in your hometown.

You and your boyfriend—a city boy who has never spent much time in the wild—go on a camping trip in the Sierras. During the middle of the night, you hear some commotion outside the tent. You peer out to see a bear at your nearby picnic table, sitting on the ground eating your sandwiches. Your boyfriend is at first paralyzed with fear, then becomes frantic and starts packing everything up to leave. What happens next?

If you could trade lives with someone for a week, who would it be? Why?

The newly elected pope is a woman. How did this come to pass?

List your favorite songs. Use a line from one of the songs as the first line of a scene.

Happy Families Are Not All Alike.

Think about the worst thing that has ever happened to you. What elements leading up to the event would you change if you could? How would the outcome have been different?

....

....

....

....

....

Write about a time in your life when you narrowly escaped some terrible fate—but change the ending, and write as if the terrible thing actually happened.

....

....

....

....

....

....

Your children aren't best friends anymore.

....

....

....

....

....

....

At the zoo, a youth throws a tennis ball into the rhino enclosure. The mother rhino ingests the tennis ball and dies slowly over the course of four days, leaving behind her baby calf and stirring anguish and outrage throughout the nation. Tell the youth's story.

Think about someone you see every day—a neighbor walking the dog, the mailman, a school crossing guard—but never talk to. Write a scene describing what one of them has been doing up until the moment he or she sees you.

Yesterday, you landed in a foreign country. Today, you wake up on a park bench with nothing but the clothes on your back. The last thing you remember is being offered a cup of juice by your driver as you were leaving the airport.

Pick a favorite character from literature, then imagine him/her/it
at your family's dinner table during the holidays.

List five favorite smells, and what they remind you of.

Write an Internet dating profile for a character in a story.
Where does he or she lie or exaggerate?

You look out the window and discover a body floating face down in your pool.

Someone is following you. Who is it? What does the person want?

Develop an obsession—hoarding, shopping, counting parking meters.
Now write about it in a way that makes it seem pleasurable.

Describe the most hideous outfit you've ever seen. Now imagine
that someone you hate is wearing it, and looks amazing. What do
you say to compliment him or her?

Breaking news: The government has banned caffeine. What are
doctors advising folks to do to stay alert, and why? Write the
television news segment.

You receive a mysterious message from outer space.
What does it say?

Outline four points of the platform for your "third party"
candidate.

You are at an outdoor recital. A noise disturbs the performance.
Describe what you were listening to, and the sound of the
interruption.

What would you do if you weren't afraid?

Someone close to you has died. After they die, you witness a
sign that there is an afterlife or something "beyond." What
do you witness?

You're twelve, and you just saw aliens break your big sister's bike. Your parents are going to think you did it. Convince them that it was the aliens.

Your best friend is having an affair with a married man whom you detest. You decide to try to end it by writing an anonymous e-mail to the man's wife.

Police raid the house next door and find drugs, drug dealers, and a live pet jaguar.

What's the biggest misconception about you? Write the truth of the matter.

After the rioting seemed to have ended, our hunger got the best of us, and we ventured out for some pizza. . . .

Write the dialogue between two neighbors chatting about the weather. One is modest and the other is pompous. They despise each other, but are too polite to let on.

Write for 10 minutes. Include in your story a video arcade, snowflakes, and a lost dog.

Write a 400-word story featuring alligator boots, the aroma of baking bread, and disappointment.

From the point of view of a teacher, write a five-sentence report card for yourself when you were . . . eight.

. . . 11.

. . . 15.

. . . 18.

What is the characteristic you hated about yourself as a child
that you've grown to appreciate, and what was the moment when you
realized it was OK?

You take one look at the note from your landlord and you decide to
move out on the spot. What does the note say?

Explain why you stayed with someone you didn't love.

You arrive at your sister's home in Grand Rapids, Michigan, after not having seen her for five years. She lives in a small cottage by herself, and when she opens the door, you realize she is a hoarder; the cottage is filled with stuff from floor to ceiling.

What's the most prominent sensation your body is feeling right now? Where is it, and how does it feel?

You're in a room with a half-open door. There's a party going on in the rest of the house. Describe what you hear.

You are the accomplished chair of a university writing department, and your
16-year-old daughter tells you she has failed English.

Describe a product that hasn't been invented yet.

Write five messages from the Ouija board.

Write a note to the teenagers who left pizza boxes and beer cans
on the floor of the family room.

Write a letter to your landlord about the noise you've been
hearing upstairs.

Going through the airport security line

Write an ode to the junk food you ate as a child.

You're locked in your favorite department store overnight.

Go to Craigslist and browse the Personals. Choose one ad; imagine the person who wrote it. Write one story in which the ad is successful, and the person meets his or her ideal match. Or write a story in which someone answers the ad, but disaster ensues.

A small ship is sailing around the world with only the captain and a passenger on board. At each port, the captain must leave the passenger and pick up another. Who are these people?

Come up with the name of a new nail polish color, and describe the type of woman who would wear it.

It's the 4th of July. At the end of a fireworks display in Washington, DC, something goes
terribly wrong. What is it? What happens next?

Describe a time when you thought you had reached your physical
limit, only to surpass it.

Describe a time when quitting was the right decision, even though
it hurt your pride.

Make a list of ingredients for a recipe. All the ingredients must be inedible.

Pity the young ones.

You've fallen in love with a member of the opposite political party. Write the breakup scene.

I will never need to experience . . .

Write about a chance encounter at a cemetery.

Explain death to a three-year-old.

Explain why humans are superior to jellyfish.

Your dream house

Your safe place

Write a story in the third person, revealing the one thing about
yourself you don't want people to know.

I had no time to be afraid.

I think I'm in the wrong room.

I kept walking, but I
knew I would stop before
I got there.

I'm not built for this kind
of thing anymore.

The nicest thing anyone has ever
said to you

Facebook has suddenly shut down your
account due to the content of your last
post. What was the post?

The night Osama bin Laden was killed,
what was the scene at the White House
from Michelle Obama's point of view?

A postcard love letter

When did you taste something you thought you hated, only to change
your mind and decide you liked it?

Describe a meal that forever changed the way you eat.

What was the strangest thing you ever ate, and how did you react?

Why haven't they gotten married?

You are a dignitary visiting a foreign country. You are presented with a strange dish that you must eat or risk offending your host. Describe the food—what it looks like, smells like, and tastes like—and the way you eat it.

This is what I want you to know about me.

That was a lie. *This* is what I want you to know about me.

You are sleeping with your fiancée in a tent on a remote beach in Nicaragua. In the middle of the night, you hear what sounds like thousands of hands beating on the tent. When you unzip the flap and look outside, all you see is an empty beach.

You see two little girls in the playground and can tell that one of them will get nearly everything she wants from life, while the other will suffer endless disappointments and frustrations. What are the signs you see?

_____

_____

_____

_____

_____

_____

_____

_____

Now: what can you tell the second little girl that will help her change the course of her life?

_____

_____

_____

_____

_____

_____

_____

_____

_____

Write a birth scene with an unexpected twist.

Write a death scene with an unexpected twist.

Write an epitaph of no more than four
lines for a chapter in your life that
is now closed.

You have been given the opportunity to
atone for one sin. Which is it, and how
do you atone?

That time you almost drowned

Describe what you wore on the first day
of school in eighth grade.

Write a letter to your grandchildren.

A 50-year-old man pulls into a gas station to use the john. A piece of graffiti
on the wall of the stall makes him turn around and head back in the direction
he came from. What did the graffiti say? Where is he going?

You are the first human to land on an alien planet. What do you
see? What is the first thing you want to ask the aliens about
their world?

You've decided to propose to your high-maintenance
boyfriend/girlfriend.

You wake up from a vivid dream and realize that something
is different.

Write a Facebook post about your day, one year from now.

_____
_____
_____
_____
_____
_____
_____
_____
_____

Write a Facebook post as if you lived on the opposite side of the
world. What are you doing there?

_____
_____
_____
_____
_____
_____
_____
_____
_____
_____

It's noon. You are walking down a boulevard in Los Angeles near the courthouse, and you come upon a body lying in the gutter. You don't know if the person is dead or alive.

You've let your eager and well-meaning eight-year-old niece believe that she's your intern. But she's doing a terrible job. What do you say when you "fire" her?

You find a to-do list you wrote when you were 10 years old. What's on it?

Go to a flea market, and write the stories of the treasures you see.

Where do you least want to be? Describe someone living there every day for the rest of his or her life.

Shots rang out.

Steve Jobs meets Thomas Edison. What do they talk about?

A construction worker's boot sits alone on the side of the highway.

Write a 12-line poem whose lines begin with words that start with
the letters R, V, H, O, K, E. Use each letter twice.

Try it again, but this time, make every other line rhyme.

A place from the past

Describe a downtown intersection
through the eyes of . . . an architect.

. . . a surfer.

. . . a thief.

. . . a parking attendant.

Write a newspaper headline
(no more than seven words) that
describes your . . . childhood.

. . . first kiss.

. . . job interview.

. . . marriage.

Write about your preferred victimless crime.

Write about a crime in which you were the victim.

Hera writes a letter to Zeus regarding the time he has not been
spending around the house.

Write a letter to your coworker describing what you don't want to
see when you get back from vacation.

Write a letter to your most senior employee that justifies why he
or she is being replaced by the boss's nine-year-old son.

Should I stay or should I go?

This is your last chance to tell her what you really think . . .

A blind friend walks down your favorite street. Describe the journey through the sounds they hear.

Word-associate—meaning, one word leads to the next. Your first
word is *melancholy*. Your final word is *spoon*.

You stumbled upon the diary of your favorite historical figure—
Amelia Earhart, Benjamin Franklin, Albert Einstein—and you
discover that the history books have it all wrong.

A brief acceptance letter from the International Association of
Humorless Individuals awarding membership

Write an employee review of yourself, critiquing your performance
of your first job ever.

A televangelist has just been elected president of the United States.
Write his/her inaugural address.

Are you sorry you spent
so much money on that
experience?

Two people are in a car. They have
just committed a crime, or said "I
love you" for the first time, or
discovered that one of them is not
who he/she has pretended to be.

Ask your boss for permission to
take "paternity leave" because your
buddy's wife just had a baby.

List your lucky outfits in grade
school, high school, and now.

Write a letter to a grade-school teacher you hated. Be descriptive, specific, and detailed about what irked you and what hurt or infuriated you in your encounters.

List the places you liked to hide as a child.

Rewrite your favorite novel as a tweet of 140 characters or fewer.

The last time you're going to say it

Describe your morning rituals—the first five things you do after getting out of bed.

Write about accidentally dropping a precious object into a public trash can. What is it? How do you (or your character) get it back? Who helps? Who witnesses?

Remember someone in middle school who was teased, and how you didn't do anything to stop it. Go back to a particular moment and stand up for that child.

Sherlock Holmes opens his doors for business in your city. What mystery would you like him to solve? Write about your visit to his office.

Write about the migration of southern Floridians if sea levels have risen three feet by the year 2050, at which point Miami will be underwater and uninhabitable.

Describe the unexpected things you learned after someone close to you died.

If you could have your dream life right now, what would it be?
Describe it in detail.

Write 12 lines of dialogue spoken at the end of a long day.

Write one sentence listing five big things that happened in your life. For example, first there was the car accident, then my dad left, then I graduated. . . .

One of the people pictured in today's newspaper has a secret life that involves a member of your family. Describe how you discovered this situation.

Your car is at the mechanic's, so you rent one for the day. While loading up groceries, you open the trunk and discover a suitcase.

Write a letter to the one that got away—the girl on the subway, the guy on the plane who kept making eyes at you, the waitress whose number you were just too shy to ask for, the friend you didn't reconcile with before his tragic accident.

You're taking your freshman to college. What are the last words you say to each other before you leave his/her dorm room to get on an airplane to go home?

You swore you would not go to Thanksgiving dinner at your
cousin's house ever again if she invited her ex-boyfriend.
You go. He's there. Describe the dinner.

He's not well but he doesn't want anyone to know.
How does he hide it?

Your tender, loving, larger-than-life boyfriend makes his money
raising and fighting dogs.

You've just arrived at a parking garage ticket machine, and discover five printed receipts left by people who paid before you. They all have different times, of course, ranging from paying $26 for their ticket at 2:00 a.m. the night before, to $2 for a fifteen-minute stay at 10:30 a.m. Write five paragraphs, each one an individual story about each forgotten ticket, and about who those people are and what they were doing before coming to pay for their car.

In 2000, 118 sailors and officers died aboard the Russian submarine *Kursk*, which sank in the Barents Sea. Narrate a moment from its final hours.

What was your favorite candy when you were a child? What memory do you associate with that candy? Imagine it in your hands and in your mouth. What does it taste like and how does it make you feel?

Write an opening paragraph with only one-syllable words.

Open a newspaper and choose a person from a random article. From his
or her perspective, narrate the scene that unfolds at the breakfast
table when he or she reads this article for the first time.

Write titles for five country western or heavy metal songs.

Pick one pop song you loved as a child. Listen to it and write for at least five minutes without stopping.

What is the title of the story of your
life, written as . . . a biography?

. . . a novel?

. . . a murder-mystery?

. . . a romance?

Write the scene about the first time someone other than your family or friends told you they loved you.

Write about something you find offensive.

A couple is arguing about an empty bottle of juice with lipstick
on the rim.

Twenty-year-old Nelson Mandela time-travels to current day New
York City. What does he see?

Describe the room where the murder took place, from the point of view of the maid who cleaned it before the incident.

Describe the room where the murder took place, from the murderer's point of view.

Describe the room where the murder took place, from the victim's point of view.

It's a little-known fact that founding father Thomas Jefferson invented a rudimentary, 18th-century time machine. He uses it to travel into the future and hold US leaders accountable for what he sees as breaches of the Constitution. Pick a moment in American history and write the interaction between Jefferson and the overreaching leader.

What song do you always associate with a certain person, or a
certain relationship?

What food do you associate with a traumatic childhood event,
and why?

Choose a political issue you are passionate about, and create a character who holds the opposite view. He/she is more sympathetic and more persuasive than you. Write the dialogue of an argument between the two of you.

Narrate an uncomfortable conversation between a father and son
without using any dialogue.

Your protagonist has just accidentally hit Reply All on a
dicey e-mail at work. Now what?

"Get in," he ordered.

Take a sentence you admire from someone else's writing. (A long sentence works best.)
Mimic the sentence, copying it word for word in terms of parts of speech, but use your
own words. For every noun, article, verb, conjunction, etc., substitute your own noun,
article, verb, conjunction, etc.

People who trash public bathrooms

People who mispronounce my name

Each year, everyone's problems are solved for one day. Then they go back to their old lives. What changes about these people?

Create your "stranded on a desert island" list. The five books you'd want to have:

The five movies you'd want to have:

The five foods you'd want to have:

The five photos of loved ones you'd want to have:

Describe your current surroundings as if you were Ernest Hemingway.

Now, as if you were J. K. Rowling.

A hurtfully inappropriate present being opened—the kind that
could end a friendship.

....

....

....

....

....

A person carrying great guilt meets with a travel agent.

....

....

....

....

....

A person mistakes you for someone else, but you're not sure who.
You keep talking to find out.

....

....

....

....

....

Someone you love is struggling in a lake, about 40 feet offshore. Describe your swim to rescue them.

Your life in one word

A supermarket ad in the Sunday paper causes the supermarket's stock price to plummet on Monday morning. What does the ad say?

Write a sentence without using the letter e.

The reason you were late to your own wedding.

You sit down at a restaurant and dis-cover a dish on the menu that contains an ingredient you thought had been recalled by the manufacturer and discontinued forever. You order it, only to find . . .

Someone in your graduating high school class has set fire to the office where all the records are kept. Describe the student you most suspect.

Write five political slogans for the advancement of public nudity.

You have an opportunity to distribute an etiquette primer to every passenger on your next commercial flight. What does it say?

You are given an opportunity to step into the pages of a novel, play a character, and return to normal life in two weeks. Your choices are *Anna Karenina*, *The Great Gatsby*, and *Howards End*. Which novel would you choose, and why?

Whose approval is your character seeking?

What change does your character resist making?

The last nightmare you had

It's your 10th high school reunion. You were the unpopular kid, but now you've made millions with the sale of a few successful start-ups. Describe your interactions with your former classmates.

Nixon's deathbed

When I left the front door open that morning . . .

Write a story about a character preparing dinner for a person he/she dislikes.

Describe the daytime sounds in your childhood home.

Describe the nighttime sounds in your childhood home.

A confession

Write about a tree you climbed and what you found hidden in a big
hole on the top of the trunk.

Describe the next year of someone who just received an enormous
secret inheritance and a diagnosis of terminal stage 4 cancer on
the same day.

Describe someone receiving a gift that you made for them by hand—
and they love it.

Describe someone receiving a gift that you made for them by hand—
but they can't tell what it is.

Rewrite the description on the book jacket for *Where the Wild Things Are* as if it were . . . a young adult novel.

. . . a horror novel.

. . . literary fiction.

. . . narrative nonfiction.

You give a homeless person some change and he/she knows your name.

_____

_____

_____

_____

_____

Describe the feeling of being stung by a dozen bees.

_____

_____

_____

_____

_____

Write a letter to someone you no longer speak with.

_____

_____

_____

_____

_____

You've been accused of plagiarism, and the charges are true. Write a
letter to your editor coming clean.

Write a list of the 10 magazines you would want your guests to
find in your bathroom.

Write a list of the times you began crying uncontrollably.

Write a party scene from the perspective of the caterer who walks the
floor with a tray of hors d'oeuvres.

Take a scene from *The Godfather, Chinatown, The Wizard of Oz,* or any other classic film. Insert a character from your own fictional writing into this scene and rewrite the scene in his/her voice.

Your neighbor finds you looking through his garbage.

Your friend comes out to you, telling you he's gay. What is the
first thing you say?

A child and a very old woman are told that a bird is actually
a dinosaur. One believes this; the other does not. Write
their conversation.

Write a text message exchange between a couple that goes from romantic to breaking up. As you write, pay special attention to the turning points in the mood.

You find yourself aboard the *Titanic* with full knowledge of what
is going to happen.

You have endless financial resources available to you for one day
and you can keep only what you've purchased during those 24 hours.
How will you spend the money?

The next-door neighbor has discovered your secret.

You find yourself living in a cave for a year. Describe it.

Write about chocolate.

How did your parents
pick your name?

If you could pick another name,
what would it be and why?

What's your nickname and why?

If you could pick a new nickname
for yourself, what would it be?

Write the interior monologue of someone waiting for the bus.

Write the interior monologue of someone waiting for a blind
date to show up.

Your younger self is about to be offered your first job. What would you tell yourself, knowing what you know now?

Sit and think about your childhood room. What objects do you remember? Write down as many as you can. Then pick one, and describe where you think it is right now.

It's 1880 in the Wild West. Write a short scene in which you—the stranger in town—walk into a saloon and order a drink.

A magazine is writing an article about something that happened to you yesterday. What does the headline say?

Write a scene, using only dialogue, that depicts the worst fight
you ever got into with your spouse, friend, or relative.

Describe to a retailer why you're returning a pair of shoes
designed for walking on the Arctic Circle.

At the end of yet another failed relationship, you decide the problem must be that you are attracted to the wrong kind of person. To figure out what traits all your exes have in common—and thus what traits you should avoid—you dig up old photographs of them and lay them out on a table.

When did you last
receive an unexpected gift?

Your beloved father, who has just been
diagnosed with severe kidney disease,
asks you to lunch. At lunch, he asks
you if you will donate one of your
kidneys to him.

Write a haiku about
breakfast.

You are a pro at breaking up
with people. What's your secret?

An editor has rejected your short story. You are writing him an e-mail. What's in the subject line?

Write a thank-you note for a gift you hated.

A woman is addicted to eating cigarettes.

You have invented a private, invitation-only, online social network. What do all the members have in common?

Write a dramatic scene that takes place in a church.

What type of person makes a better leader—someone who is loved
or someone who is feared?

Write your own myth to describe what happens to people
when they die.

A dialogue between two characters in which what is not said
is more important than what is said

A scene in which a character recognizes she's being lied to

Write a commencement speech for Starfleet Academy.

Write a commencement speech for the Jedi Academy.

Write about the time you stole something—a bag of pretzels, a shirt,
an idea—from a friend.

Create a self-loathing James Bond villain. He or she strives for world domination, but what is he/she compensating for? Write a few diary entries.

What's on your mantel, and why?

Consider a news story from the past week that made you feel
impassioned, despite the fact that the central issue doesn't
impact your daily life. Write about why issues matter to us
even when they don't affect us.

You discover that you are one-quarter Cherokee.

How many times have you worn those shoes? Where've they been? With
whom? Doing what? (If you really want to have fun, write from the
shoes' point of view.)

Think of the person you hate most. What part of them exists in
you, and what does that side make you do?

The first time you were ever deceived

The first time you deceived someone

A wedding planner tries to talk a young couple into signing up for a more elaborate ceremony than they had originally planned.

I met him on the stairs.

List ten places you'd rather
be right now.

Write directions for how
to get from your house to
the nearest supermarket.

What was the hardest thing
you've ever had to forgive?

A child comes over to a friend's house and compares her home life to
the friend's home life.

Write for 10 minutes without stopping about everything that stops you
from writing.

You wake up, and everyone in your family is gone. There's a Post-it on the kitchen counter. What does it say?

Narrate the best one minute you can imagine.

Steve Jobs comes back to life and invents one more groundbreaking product. What is it? Come up with a tagline that Apple will use to sell it.

You are asked to write a blurb for a biography of your best friend.

You have just been handed five million dollars to start your own company, doing whatever you are passionate about. What is it? What do you do first? What do you do second?

You receive a phone call from a grown son whom you gave up for adoption and
who never wanted any connection to you. He says he wants you to meet your
granddaughters.

Your daughter was born without taste buds. One day, she asks you to describe the experience of eating a butterscotch sundae. What do you tell her?

Your new love, an accomplished fiction writer, is coming to your house for dinner for the first time. Earlier today, you bought 20 new books to display, hoping to impress him. Write the dialogue for the scene when he discovers you've never read them.

A character gets a flat tire and calls AAA. The person who shows up in the tow truck is someone they knew long ago. Who is it? What happens?

The last man you spoke to has just been approached by a fortune-teller who tells him that he must give up his dreams or else he will turn to stone. What does he do?

A note to a Broadway actor asking him or her to meet after the evening's performance

You're James Joyce pretending to be F. Scott Fitzgerald. Write a sentence or two.

Now you're F. Scott Fitzgerald pretending to be James Joyce.

Imagine a movie by one film director redone by a film director with a completely different style. For example, Woody Allen tackles *Star Wars*. Tim Burton remakes *The Godfather*. Quentin Tarantino takes on *Midnight Cowboy*.

Take the last line of your favorite story you have written and use it
as the beginning of a new story.

Randomly choose five
books off your shelf.
Retitle them.

Did you have a special place that
brought you comfort as a child—
somewhere you went to feel safe?
Describe the place, and the
feelings it aroused in you.

What does dripping water
from a faucet sound like?

It turns out George W. Bush
is an avid painter of dogs.
Narrate his inner monologue
as he works on one of his
paintings.

Write 20 lines of dialogue between a believer and a nonbeliever.

You're on a bus. Your ex-boyfriend, whom you haven't seen in 10 years, gets on at the next stop. He sits down in the seat in front of you, not recognizing who you are.

What you see in the clouds

Write about a situation in which an organ recipient becomes obsessed with the organ donor.

You find another version of your grandmother's will in a hidden desk drawer.

You've been hired to write a one-minute-long play that involves two brothers, a robbery, and a love affair.

A close friend has just sent you a suicide note by text.
What are the next 10 text exchanges?

Describe the one thing your parents own that you and each of your siblings are secretly hoping to inherit.

You received a robot in the mail, but the instructions are missing. Write the instructions.

You discover a photo of your grandmother standing next to a young man who is not your grandfather. Who is he, and what does the caption say?

This is what my life looks like when everybody is watching.

This is what my life looks like when nobody is watching.

Describe the last time you wished you had a camera, but didn't.

Deconstruct your favorite film.

You are a newspaper reporter, and a high-ranking White House official leaks you a top government secret. What is it? Write the first five paragraphs of the article.

You're answering a personal ad and
your prospective date wants to know
in two short sentences what kind of
toothpaste you use, and why.

Describe a big disappointment
that turned out to be better for
you in the long run.

A man hires a private investigator
to locate his wife, who has
disappeared. The investigator
disappears soon after.

The tumor is benign.

Two people meet in an airport bar. Each is waiting to pick up an
unaccompanied minor at a nearby gate. Write the dialogue.

Write five minutes of copy for a TV news feature about speed dating.

Describe what a person falling from a great height is thinking in the last the two or three seconds of his or her life.

_____

_____

_____

_____

_____

Write about someone learning something shocking from an obituary.

_____

_____

_____

_____

_____

_____

You find a suitcase with an ID tag that reads, "These are the only things she saved." What's inside?

_____

_____

_____

_____

_____

_____

Invent a disease. Write
an ad for the cure.

The most ragged piece of
clothing in your closet,
and why you've kept it all
these years

If you were a fascist
dictator, you'd begin
your reign by . . .

Describe a magic trick in a
way that doesn't give away
its secret.

Your support group doesn't support your resignation from your support group.

A valedictorian of a high school class has to be taken offstage in the middle of her speech. What happened?

Google "sergeant's drill hat" and view the images that turn up. Describe what you see. Now describe someone wearing one.

Your best friend has to choose between you and his/her significant other.
Why are you the better choice?

Your first concert

Out of character

You realize you can understand a
surprising amount of a foreign language,
despite having never studied it.
Then you discover why.

The door wouldn't lock.

The advice Hippocrates gives Achilles about his vulnerable ankle.

You have a desperate crush on your barista, but you've never talked about anything other than how you like your latte. Describe how you take it to the next level.

You happen upon the blog of one of your writing students, and you realize he/she has been stalking you.

Outline the sequel to Shakespeare's *Romeo and Juliet*.

Outline the sequel to Jane Austen's *Pride and Prejudice.*

You are breaking up with a girlfriend/boyfriend of several years. What are the last three lines of your final letter to him/her?

Write about the act of kissing someone without naming a body part.

You are in a foreign country. You keep saying a word that you thought meant "please" but actually means "idiot." Explain yourself to the person you just offended.

The milk from your corner store is curdled, again.

You've finally decided to end your relationship with your abusive mother.
Write her the letter that cuts ties.

Think of your most embarrassing moment. Write it from the perspective
of someone who witnessed it.

A scene in which a character is seasick

You have been asked to design a T-shirt to support your favorite cause. What will your T-shirt say?

Write a story that plays out through a series of YouTube videos.

Let's say there's no Heaven, no Hell, and no Purgatory. There are, however, two distinct subdivisions of the afterlife, with a third area that enables souls to move from one to another. Describe them.

Write a story that ends with: She wiped the knife clean on his bedspread.

You are watching Barbara Walters sit down for a one-on-one interview with President Obama. What is one subject they will discuss? Write a few minutes of the interview.

Put three characters who don't like each other in a room together,
and start writing.

Put a Michelin-starred chef in a marriage with a husband who is
addicted to junk food, and start writing.

Your boss has to fire half of your team. Why should she keep you?
Why should she fire you?

You are in graduate school, and you realize you've fallen in love with your professor.

To draw attention to your company, you invent a compelling cofounder and trick online reporters into writing about this imaginary person. Soon there are insistent requests to interview him or her on television. What happens next?

Write the longest run-on sentence you can about one of the happiest moments or days or events of your life.

Write a haiku about your underwear.

Write a poem about pizza.

Identify the most minor character from your favorite novel, and tell his or her story.

Write about yourself as seen by a total stranger walking toward
you on the sidewalk.

You are serving on the jury for a domestic violence case, and you realize
that you have a lot in common with the plaintiff—namely, that you have
suffered a similar kind of abuse and that the codependent relationship
in question is similar to the one you're currently in.

As Robert Frost wrote, "Two roads diverged in a yellow wood." What
does the sign at the intersection say?

Describe the hands of your beloved.

BREAKING NEWS

Should we interpret the Constitution the way our founding fathers intended, or should we interpret it based on changing social circumstances?

Describe a game of hide-and-seek when no one finds you.

Your pen just came to life. The first thing it says is . . .

You are a famous actor being interviewed by a bright young reporter about a movie you've just made. You thought the script was lousy. You had a terrible time on set with the director. You dated and dumped your costar. You start the interview praising the film but gradually the truth slips out. Write the scene from the beginning.

Activists are campaigning to remove a color from the rainbow. Which color, and what's their argument?

Zeus and his daughter Athena are living in 21st-century San Francisco. Describe a conversation between them at the dinner table.

The worst date of your life

Name all the places in a house where family members hide things from one another.

Write in the voice of a wise 11-year-old about the misdeeds of a parent
or other relative.

The day after a birthday party for a 100-year-old.

You wake up in jail and don't know why you're there. You find three
items in your pocket, and slowly your memory returns.

Think about a memorable vacation. What would have happened if
you'd decided to stay and never return home?

If Facebook had existed, what status update would the Wright Brothers have posted after their first successful flight?

You see a UFO in the sky. What does your tweet say?

You are about to move across the world for a job and someone treats you to a farewell dinner at a Chinese restaurant. What does your fortune cookie say?

You're tapped by a super-secret government organization to usher an extraterrestrial through a day in the life of an average American. Starting with the moment you open your eyes in the morning, it's your job to tell this creature what it is people do, and why. As part of your official duties, you must produce a written account of the interaction.

You've been standing in line for an hour in the exact same spot.
Describe your body and how it feels.

Your son is addicted to modern technology and insists on
interacting with the world solely through gadgets and the
Internet. You can't even operate a cell phone.

His wrists still hurt where the handcuffs had been.

If you could solve one world problem, what would it be, and why?

A letter you mailed more than 10 years ago appears in your mailbox marked "Return to sender." Who is it addressed to? What's inside? And why was it returned?

Write the professional biography that your younger self imagined you'd have today.

Waiting for the kiss to stop

You take a big bite of a juicy burger and, as you're chewing, you spot a long hair entwined in the patty. What happens next?

Write, as a timeline, the five most important moments of the last week/month/year.

A 65-year-old man has lost his job and all his money and now lives in a van with his dog.
He writes a letter to his daughter. What does it say?

The person she hates the most in the world

The person she loves most in the world

Recall an old childhood photo. Narrate the events that led up to the moment that photo was taken.

You see a twenty-something guy wearing earbuds and laughing hard.
What's so funny?

Now make him old.

You are a marine being awarded the Medal of Honor for your role in
a battle abroad. Describe the battle.

_____

_____

_____

_____

_____

_____

_____

_____

_____

Describe the battle from the point of view of the local farmer
who witnessed it.

_____

_____

_____

_____

_____

_____

_____

_____

_____

_____

Write the advertising copy for a high-end face cream made from a secret ingredient you can't disclose, but which makes your product better than anything anyone's ever used.

Recall a plea your teenage self made to your parents. Write it now as an adult.

Describe the tense mood in a courtroom just before the verdict is delivered.

An out-of-the-office vacation e-mail that describes specific places and times you'll be checking e-mail

Two friends have trekked for two days to a backcountry campsite. They
are alone and realize on the second night that their food supply has been
spoiled. What is the conversation that night as the temperature drops?

Take your favorite film, novel, or story and write a summary of
it. Now completely change the characters, time frame, setting,
etc., and rewrite the summary, keeping the story line intact.

You read an article titled "Four Under One." What is it about?

You have one chance to communicate with someone much loved who
has passed on.

....

....

....

....

....

....

....

Your dad crossed the Grand Canyon on a tightrope and you're
terrified of heights.

....

....

....

....

....

....

....

Go have dinner at your favorite restaurant. Now pick a famous
person you've never met and describe the dinner as if that
person had been there and eaten it.

....

....

....

....

....

....

When was a moment when you realized you were braver than you
thought you could be?

_____

_____

_____

_____

_____

_____

_____

_____

_____

When did you realize the person you used to be in love with was
wrong for you?

_____

_____

_____

_____

_____

_____

_____

_____

_____

_____

Write in the voice of an 80-year-old man who just discovered a big family secret after finding a letter in his attic.

When did someone turn out to be completely different from what you first thought? How did that change you?

Write instructions for how to tie a bow.

While flying first class to LA, you learn that you're sitting next to the creator of your favorite TV show. What do you say to him/her?

On a different flight, you learn that you're sitting next to the creator of your least favorite TV show. What do you say to him/her?

Describe the process of making a peanut butter and jelly sandwich to a creature from another planet who doesn't know what bread, or a knife, or a refrigerator is.

Who or what would you be in another life?

You have been blind since birth. A doctor invents a pill that will allow you sight for precisely 24 hours. Where would you go? What would you do? Whom would you choose to see?

The coldest you've ever been

Write a letter of forgiveness to someone unforgivable.

An elderly friend is dying. He begins to dictate to you a letter of forgiveness to his son, from whom he's been estranged for 50 years. You have the son's name and address but your friend passes away before the letter has been finished. In a few sentences, complete the letter to the son, explaining how you knew his father.

During a hike in the wilderness, you stumble upon an old-timey
religious revival at the bank of a river. You duck down behind
a tree. What is the leader saying to his/her flock?

You're in Las Vegas and you see your favorite celebrity at a
nightclub doing something extremely offensive.

The biggest difference between me and the person sitting
next to me is . . .

A person from a parallel universe manifests in your doorway. The person's life is the total opposite of yours. The person's beliefs are . . .

The person eats . . .

The person wears . . .

The person never . . .

Rewrite a story you have written, cutting the word count in half.

You put a letter to yourself in a time capsule twenty years ago.
What does it say?

Describe something you did that you knew was wrong, and your
rationalization for it.

You are a superhero. Your special power is the ability to walk
through walls, pass through solid objects, and hide inside solid
materials. What is your backstory, and how did you get this
special power?

A father picks out a gift for an adolescent child he hasn't seen in a year.

New Year's Eve in Reykjavík

One of your grandparents tells you something important.

How do you get yourself back to sleep in the middle of the night?

Write about someone who has collected thousands of the same item. What item is it, why collect it, and how does the collection affect this person's life?

Your home country has dissolved. Write a letter to the president
of the new country where you want to live, explaining why you want
to live there.

Write the encyclopedic entry of your now-vanished country,
explaining what happened.

You're stranded on a desert island with two pieces of paper and a pen, and no hope of being rescued. Knowing no one will ever read it, what do you write?

What you'd know, that you don't know now, if you'd grown up in _____
[insert name of foreign country]

What you'd know, that you don't know now, if you'd grown up in _____
[insert name of US state]

What you'd know, that you don't know now, if you'd been born in _____
[insert year]

Your mom—who lives three states away—just arrived with four suitcases. She tells you she's moving in.

Take life advice from your teenage self.

One major anxiety of this era

What is the most evocative smell from your childhood? Write an evocative scene to convince the reader of its significance in your life.

Will you still love me tomorrow?

In God We Trust is America's motto.
Create a new one.

He's ashamed he hasn't spoken up
about _____ so he _____.

She's ashamed she hasn't spoken up
about _____ because _____.

Describe your kid's favorite pajamas and what it took to get him or her into bed.

Write a page of scene, then compress it down to half a page, then to a quarter of a page, then to just one sentence, whittling down the drama to its bare essence.

An act of sabotage

You die and come back to life for just one minute to tell one person that there actually is an afterlife. Who do you tell, and what do you say?

Describe an act of revenge you performed against someone who never knew it was you.

How do you cut an apple?

As you approach your car, a parking attendant is placing a ticket on your windshield.

There are 50 people left on earth. You each have a specific role. What is your role?

Open your junk mail and read it, then reply to each as if writing to an old friend.

Explain to your tenant what that red stain actually is . . .

In a writing workshop setting, there's usually a person whose work and overall demeanor you cannot stand. Write the first paragraph of the short story brought in by that person for group critique.

Invent the most high-calorie fast-food sandwich of all time, and name it.

Write about a recreational hike that turns into a struggle for survival.

Write about one pivotal moment from your childhood that, had it gone
differently, would have changed your life choices entirely.

The house you lived in when you were six years old

Write about arriving late to the Full Moon party.

You accompany your mother on an errand to the pharmacy, and as you exit the store, a security guard pulls your mother aside and arrests her for shoplifting some cosmetics. He pulls out the cosmetics from her bag, and you know she didn't pay for them.

A creative writing teacher fears that a student is more talented than she is.
Write a scene in which she critiques a story the student has written.

This is how I got lost in the wild.

What is lint, really?

Watch your favorite romantic comedy. Rewrite the last scene so that the main characters don't end up together, and set it in the same environment as your favorite science fiction flick.

Describe what you've always wished were different about your body.

Describe what you most love about your body, in generous detail.

Write a list of five melodies that immediately evoke a specific memory of a person and place.

What's in your character's glove compartment? Medicine cabinet? Bedside drawer?

Open a piece of story with: "I steal."

A man learns to ride a bicycle at age 50.

Write about someone who joins the army of another country for
idealistic reasons.

Creatures live under your fingernails. Who are they?

A 10th circle has been added to Dante's *Inferno*. Describe it.

Write yourself into a major event in history—the Nanking Massacre, the Kennedy White House during the Cuban missile crisis in 1962, the stock market crash of 1929, the bubonic plague in Europe, for example—and tell a story that is personal (as opposed to historical), using the historical backdrop simply for setting and texture. Try writing it as a series of letters or journal entries.

"First impressions aren't always what they seem." Write about the first time this expression rang true for you.

A friendly neighbor whose child is best friends with your own is
picked up on suspicion of planning a suicide bombing.

You're in a very happy marriage. One day your husband—also the
father of your children—goes to work and never returns home.

Photocopy five poems and cut out the verses. Rearrange them to inspire a new story. Write it here.

Your main character heads to the airport to begin a two-week trip.
What's the one most important thing in his or her bags?

Narrate your first kiss, using no adjectives.

The last woman you spoke to just won a million dollars, but she said no to the money. Why?

Your mother reveals that your biological father is a world-famous inventor who never acknowledged you as his daughter. You decide to contact him.

Consider what you're wearing right at this moment. Describe how each piece of clothing came into your life.

Two bored FBI agents are discussing your e-mail. Write 10 lines of dialogue that begin with, "Wait a minute, Jake, I think I found something."

A personal ad you'd never want
to respond to

Albert Woolson, the last surviving Union
army veteran of the Civil War, lived
until 1956. Write a scene in which he
flies on a jumbo jet for the first time.

You've created a new miracle drug that
can, literally, perform any miracle,
except . . .

Why can't you be fenced in?

Your dream marriage proposal

Just days after trying out for
Manchester United Football Club, a
20-year-old man is involved in a
motorcycle accident and paralyzed
from the chest down.

Imagine a drawer. Open it.
List 10 things you discover inside.

You're 17. Explain why you couldn't
finish your homework last night.

Write about allergies.

America's last squirrel has just been stuffed and mounted for Smithsonian display next to the long-extinct passenger pigeon. How would a museum tour guide describe the events leading to the species' extinction?

Write about a celebrity obsession.

Your biggest regret of the day so far

When they came back from the party, someone had broken into the apartment.

A window washer spies someone on a nearby ledge.

Write dialogue for a family of four in a car on vacation.

Write 12 lines of dialogue spoken in anger.

You are going on a sailing trip and can only take absolute essentials—
a bathing suit, underwear, two changes of clothes, two changes of
shoes. You are allowed one discretionary item, but it must fit into
a small cubbyhole under your berth. What will you take?

A scam artist eats his way to 700 pounds with a scheme to lose the
weight and become a millionaire, motivational, weight-loss guru.
But, having successfully made himself morbidly obese, he finds he
cannot control the monster he's made.

Select a random book from your shelf and turn to page 53. Use the first full sentence that appears on that page as the first sentence of a new story.

Journalists brag that they can write 100 words about their big toe. Write 100 words about your big toe.

While folding laundry after two weeks away from home on a business trip, you discover a piece of black bikini underwear that isn't yours—and isn't your husband's, either.

The photograph I can't live without

Describe the facial expression of a city bus driver whose last passenger of the day hands her a copy of the Qur'an.

Write a list of the 10 things you would most love to find
at a garage sale.

Write a list of the 10 locations, real or imagined, to which you
would like to be beamed from the Starship *Enterprise*.

Write about America as a freshly defected North Korean.

Write a false epiphany—the sort where a character thinks he's
figured it all out but hasn't.

You've finally had enough of your inner child. Write the note you
leave on the nightstand telling him or her you're leaving for
good. But don't be too hurtful.

The recently inducted leader of North Korea, Kim Jong-un, has a sudden change of heart. He gives all his soldiers leave, opens the border to South Korea, and puts a Gone Fishing sign on his door. Write a few breaking-news reports he hears/sees from his rental property on Lake Como.

Curling? Really? Eliminate an Olympic sport—and make the case for a new one.

Find the narrative thread in the song names of the Billboard Hot 100 and the titles on the *New York Times* best-seller list.

Everyone leaves Earth because of something someone said.
What was said?

A woman travels continents and oceans to be at her dying father's
bedside and when he doesn't die, even though she loves him, she's
disappointed. Why?

What you're most afraid of in the world

Open *Aesop's Fables* and choose one. Model a human character on each of the animals in one fable—the ant and the grasshopper, or the tortoise and the hare—giving the person the traits of each animal and revealing the story's moral through character action and speech.

The last conversation you had in an elevator

The best or worst comment you overheard on a bus

Write a pitch for the worst (or most shameless) reality TV show ever.

You're eloping. Write the note you leave for your parents on the kitchen table.

You are granted a meeting with God. You choose to ask Him to explain one of the great inhumanities in history. How does the conversation go?

Describe a trip around your high school using
only smells and touch.

_____

_____

_____

_____

_____

_____

Imagine that everyone and everything you encounter today is giving you a message
about your life. Interpret what you hear on the bus or at work, or what you see on
a billboard while driving to work as specific messages speaking directly to you
about your life. What message is the world giving you?

_____

_____

_____

_____

_____

_____

Describe the sensation of falling asleep at the end of a long day.

_____

_____

_____

_____

_____

_____

List 30 things you want to do before you die.

There's a sign at the gate to Heaven. What does it say?

There's a sign at the gate to Hell. What does it say?

Write out a dramatic event from your childhood from the perspective
of a passerby who stumbled upon the drama.

Your mother tells you she's been offered a three-minute stand-up spot at an upcoming comedy showcase. Write her opening joke.

_____

_____

_____

_____

_____

_____

You're a teenager, and your mother, who is a novelist, writes a best-seller about a terrible teenager who sounds a lot like you.

_____

_____

_____

_____

_____

_____

You've just been hit by a car and are lying on the asphalt. All you know about your condition is that your head really hurts. Record your thoughts.

_____

_____

_____

_____

_____

_____

Write about two people who share the same name showing up to
claim a prize.

Write about two people who share the same name showing up to claim
a restaurant reservation.

12 hours in the life of a zombie

12 hours in the life of a vampire

These are the very last words you will ever write.